WHAT REALLY HAPPENED?

The True Story of
CHRISTOPHER COLUMBUS

Susanna Keller

PowerKiDS press.

New York

Published in 2013 by The Rosen Publishing Group, Inc.
29 East 21st Street, New York, NY 10010

First Edition

Editor: Jennifer Way
Book Design: Colleen Bialecki

Photo Credits: Cover, p. 5 Superstock/Getty Images; p. 7 maudranos/Shutterstock.com; p. 9 Leif Eriksson Discovers America/Dahl, Hans (1849–1937)/Private Collection/Photo © O. Vaering/The Bridgeman Art Library; p. 11 Columbus Before the Queen, 1843/Leutze Emanuel Gottlieb/Brooklyn Museum of Art, New York, USA/Dick S. Ramsey Fund and Healy Purchase Fund B/The Bridgeman Art Library; p. 13 English School/Bridgeman Art Library/ Getty Images; p. 15 Rafa Irusta/Shutterstock.com; p. 17 © iStockphoto.com/Patryck Kosmider; p. 19 Capture of the Chief Caonabo on Hispaniola, Spanish School (19th century)/Private Collection/© Look and Learn/The Bridgeman Art Library; p. 21 iStockphoto/Thinkstock.

Library of Congress Cataloging-in-Publication Data

Keller, Susanna.
The true story of Christopher Columbus / by Susanna Keller. — 1st ed.
    p. cm. — (What really happened?)
Includes index.
ISBN 978-1-4488-9692-9 (library binding) — ISBN 978-1-4488-9842-8 (pbk.) —
ISBN 978-1-4488-9843-5 (6-pack)
1. Columbus, Christopher—Travel—Juvenile literature. 2. America—Discovery and exploration—Spanish—Juvenile literature. I. Title.
E118.K45 2013
970.01'5092—dc23
[B]
                                              2012028711

Manufactured in the United States of America

CPSIA Compliance Information: Batch #W13PK4. For Further Information contact Rosen Publishing, New York, New York at 1-800-237-9932

CONTENTS

HISTORY OR STORY?

You probably know stories about how Christopher Columbus "discovered" America. Maybe you learned the words "In fourteen hundred ninety-two, Columbus sailed the ocean blue." Columbus did make a journey across the Atlantic Ocean in 1492. After his voyages, the peoples of North and South America and Europe would shape each other's future.

Not every story about Columbus is true, though. He didn't have to convince everyone around him that the world was round. People already knew that. Also, Native Americans had been living in the lands he "discovered" for tens of thousands of years.

This famous portrait of Christopher Columbus was done after his death. There are no known portraits that were done while he was alive.

THE WEAVER'S SON

Christopher Columbus was born in 1451 in Genoa, in what is now Italy. His mother was Susanna Fontanarossa and his father was Domenico Colombo, a weaver and wool **merchant**. "Columbus" is the English form of "Colombo," so Christopher Columbus was known as Cristoforo Colombo in Italian.

We know little about Columbus's childhood. Genoa was a **port**, so he likely heard sailors telling stories about their trips. As a young man, Columbus became a sailor. He traveled to northern Europe and along the coast of Africa. He studied **geography** and learned to make maps. In 1479, he married Filipa Moniz Perestrelo. Their son, Diego, was born in 1480.

Christopher Columbus grew up in the port city of Genoa, Italy. Here is what that city looks like today.

THE AGE OF EXPLORATION

In 1476, Columbus settled in Portugal. Portuguese sailors were known for their **navigation** skills. They led the European **exploration** of Africa in the 1400s. Columbus learned navigation and became interested in exploration. He read about Marco Polo's trip to China in 1275 and the riches Polo described there.

Columbus guessed that if he sailed far enough west, he would end up in the rich lands he had read about. He didn't know that the Vikings, a seafaring people from northern Europe, found land when they sailed west around 1000 and had even founded a settlement in what is now Canada.

This painting shows Viking explorer Leif Eriksson landing in North America, about 500 years before Columbus's voyage.

FERDINAND AND ISABELLA

In Columbus's day, the only known route to Asia from Europe was over land. The trip took a long time. Many explorers were trying to find a quicker route.

Columbus was sure he could reach Asia by sailing across the Atlantic. He would need a ruler to back him and fund the journey, though. When the king of Portugal turned him down, he moved to Spain. Spain's rulers, Ferdinand and Isabella, were busy fighting a war against the Moors, who controlled parts of Spain. Columbus spent seven years trying to win their support before they agreed to back his voyage in 1492.

This painting shows Christopher Columbus asking Ferdinand and Isabella to fund his trip. They turned him down at least twice before agreeing to support him.

COLUMBUS'S BOATS

Despite stories that spread later, Isabella did not **pawn** her jewels to pay for Columbus's voyage. Bankers contributed some money, as did Columbus himself. Three ships were outfitted, or prepared, for the trip. The largest was the *Santa María*, which was a kind of boat called a **carrack**. Columbus rented the boat, which had been used for trading. It became his **flagship**, or the head ship for his journey.

The two smaller ships, the *Niña* and the *Pinta*, were **caravels**. They had both been trading ships before they were outfitted for Columbus's journey.

This picture shows Columbus's ships during their journey across the Atlantic Ocean.

THE FIRST VOYAGE

Columbus's ships set sail on August 3, 1492. Between them, the ships carried about 90 men. Most were Spanish sailors. The ships stopped in the Canary Islands, off the coast of Africa, for fresh food and headed west into the unknown. After several weeks at sea, many sailors wanted to turn around.

On October 12, they sighted land. Columbus named the first island he landed on San Salvador, though the people living there called it Guanahani. Today, nobody is sure which island it was! Columbus had actually reached the Caribbean islands but believed that he was in Asia.

This map shows the route Columbus took on his first voyage.

COLUMBUS'S FIRST VOYAGE, 1492

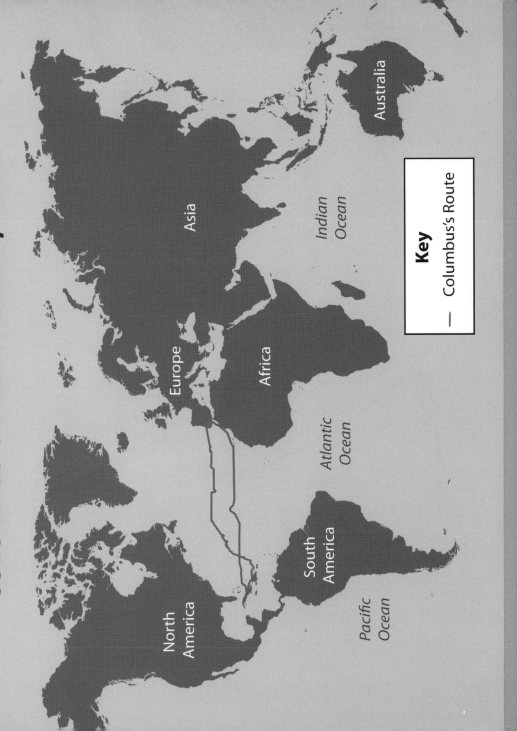

Asia

Europe

Africa

Indian
Ocean

Australia

Atlantic
Ocean

North
America

South
America

Pacific
Ocean

Key
— Columbus's Route

LATER VOYAGES

After the *Santa María* ran aground, the other ships returned to Europe. Bad weather forced Columbus to land in Portugal. He had trouble getting back to Spain. When he finally reached the Spanish court, he convinced them to send him back to what he still believed was Asia.

On September 24, 1493, he set sail with 17 ships. He planned to **conquer** the native people and start Spanish settlements. The Europeans fought with the native peoples and argued among themselves. Columbus returned to Spain but came back to the Caribbean in 1498 and 1502. He continued to think it was eastern Asia.

Christopher Columbus and his crew explored several Caribbean islands, like the one shown here. He named one of these islands Tortuga, the Spanish word for "turtle," because it reminded him of a turtle's shell.

DISCOVERY OR DISASTER?

Each time Columbus returned to Europe, he took things back with him. He brought turkeys, parrots, tobacco, and gold. He also brought native people whom he had captured and **enslaved.** After Columbus and other Europeans reached the Americas, they killed or enslaved many of the native people. Many others died from diseases that they caught from the Europeans.

While the Spanish wanted riches from the lands Columbus explored, they also hoped to convert native peoples to Christianity. The Europeans sometimes argued that this made up for the harm they caused, even though many native people were not eager to convert.

This picture shows Christopher Columbus and his men capturing a chief on the island of Hispaniola. They are doing this because they want to keep him from leading his people in fighting them.

LATER YEARS

Ferdinand and Isabella had promised to make Columbus the governor of any lands he discovered. He governed for a time, but people thought he ruled too harshly during his third trip. His job was taken away and he was sent back to Spain. Columbus returned to the Americas one last time with Ferdinand Columbus, his son with Beatriz Enríquez de Harana. However, he could not get his position back.

Columbus died in Valladolid, Spain, on May 20, 1506. Though some stories claim otherwise, Columbus did not die penniless or in prison. He did die convinced that he had reached Asia, though.

This statue of Christopher Columbus stands in Santa Margherita, Italy.

WHAT REALLY HAPPENED?

We know a fair amount about Columbus's voyages because he described them in **logs**. We have fewer **sources** of information about other subjects, such as his family and his early life. There are almost no sources that tell about Columbus's explorations from the native people's point of view.

To this day, people argue over what Columbus accomplished. Some say he was a hero who bravely discovered new lands. Others believe that his actions shouldn't be celebrated because he and the Europeans who followed him treated Native Americans so badly. What people agree on is that he changed the world forever.

GLOSSARY

caravels (KAR-uh-velz) Small ships that had broad bows, high narrow decks, and usually three masts with sails.

carrack (KAR-ik) A ship used in the 1500s that was powered by sails.

conquer (KON-ker) To overcome something.

enslaved (en-SLAYVD) Made someone be a slave.

exploration (ek-spluh-RAY-shun) Travel through little-known land.

flagship (FLAG-ship) A ship that carries the commander of a group of ships and that flies his or her flag.

geography (jee-AH-gruh-fee) The study of Earth's weather, land, countries, people, and businesses.

logs (LOGZ) Records of day-to-day activities.

merchant (MER-chunt) Someone who owns a business that sells goods.

navigation (na-vuh-GAY-shun) The act of guiding a ship, an aircraft, or a rocket.

pawn (PAWN) To leave something in exchange for money.

port (PORT) A town or city with a harbor that ships come in and out of.

sources (SORS-ez) Things that give facts or knowledge.

INDEX

WEBSITES

Due to the changing nature of Internet links, PowerKids Press has developed an online list of websites related to the subject of this book. This site is updated regularly. Please use this link to access the list:

www.powerkidslinks.com/wrh/colum/